The Tree Jumper: Profiling a Child Molester

Darren W. Freeman

Disclaimer

© 2019

All Rights Reserved.

No part of this Book can be transmitted or reproduced in any form including print, electronic, photocopying, scanning, mechanical, or recording without prior written permission from the author.

Because of the dynamic nature of the Internet, any web addresses or links contained in this book may have changed since publication and may no longer be valid. The views expressed in this work are solely those of the author, and the author hereby claims any responsibility for them.

Table of Contents

Disclaimer 2

Foreword 6

Chapter 1 9

Child Molestation: A Brief History 9

    EarlyWritings and Public Concern 10

    Who Can Be a Child Molester? 13

    Are They Only Strangers? 15

    Are They Only Males? 15

    What About Kids? 16

    How Many in the United States? 16

    How Many in Other Countries? 18

Chapter 2 20

Profiling a Child Molester 20

    Gaining Access to Victims 27

    The Very Important Persons 29

    Places of Assault 30

    Difference Between a Pedophile and a Child Molester 30

    Can a Vigilant Parent Detect a Child Molester? 32

    Myth vs. Fact 33

Chapter 3 36
Child Sexual Abuse: Effects and Treatment 36
- The Psychological Effects of Child Sexual Abuse 36
- The Physical Effects of Child Sexual Abuse 39
- Why Do Most Victims Not Tell Someone About Being Abused? 40
- Treatment 42

Chapter 4 45
The Reality of the Deep Web 45

Chapter 5 54
Beyond Conviction 54
- The Jimmy Ryce Act 56
- The Cherish Periwinkle Case 58
- Changes Made to the Jimmy Ryce Act 60
- Penalties for Failure to Report Child Molestation 61
- to pay damages for the harm caused to due to their actions. 62
- Child Molesters in Prison 62
- Incidents in Prison 64

Scope for Rehabilitation............................ 67

Chapter 6 70

What Can We Do? 70

Protecting Our Children 70

The National Sexual Assault Hotline 73

Parting Note.. 30

Foreword

I have worked in Law Enforcement for a major part of my adult life. Chasing criminals and having them answer for their crimes was a way of life for me. Currently, I teach Criminal Law and own a Private Security Company. With so much experience at hand, I can say that I have seen plenty of crimes being committed and am familiar with criminals of all kinds.

But what is the worst kind of criminal? Is there such a thing? I believe there is, and for me, the one crime which I hated the most was child molestation. As a law enforcement officer, I have interrogated several child molesters. I have even worked as a correctional officer, which required me to baby sit them.

The substantial amount of experience I have had with these individuals has taught me one thing— a child molester is the worst kind of criminal.

This book is about profiling these monsters. I hope to educate people about the dangers these individuals pose to society, how they wreak havoc into the lives of our children, how their minds work and finally, what we can do to protect our children from them.

It's not a pleasant subject and there will be times where the reader will wish they had never read any of it, but as it is with all things… running away never solved anything. There are so many horrors in this world, many that we try to turn a blind eye to, but no more. It is time we confronted this ugly reality that so many children are exposed to every day. We must do it for them, for the ones who are too young and innocent to protect themselves from these monsters.

I hope that once you have finished reading this, you will feel better equipped in how we can protect our children and make this world a little safer for them.

Darren W. Freeman

Chapter 1

Child Molestation: A Brief History

Child molestation, also referred to as child sexual abuse, is a kind of child abuse where an adult or in some cases, an older child will abuse a child for the purpose of sexual stimulation. He or she, will engage in sexual activities with the child, sometimes by asking them and sometimes by pressuring them. Child molestation also includes indecent exposure or using children for producing child pornography.

The effects of child abuse and molestation can be incredibly traumatic and long-lasting. Victims may need psychotherapy later in life and suffer from post-traumatic stress disorder and depression.

As the American Psychological Association clearly states, children simply cannot consent to any kind of sexual activity with an adult. They do not understand the nature of sexual relations, and even if they do not show any indicators of trauma, they are still exceptionally vulnerable to these horrific acts, the repercussionsof which can last a long time.

EarlyWritings and Public Concern

Child sexual abuse has been prevalent throughout history, but it only gained public attention in the past few decades. The first published work based specifically on child sexual abuse was authored byAmbroise Tardieu, a French pathologist. He is also the pioneer of forensic medicine. Tardieu studied multiple forms of child abuse and in a study published in 1857, (Etude medico-legale sur les attentats aux moeurs, translated as Forensic study on offenses against morals), Tardieu analyzed numerous cases of molestation and sexual abuse in both females (632 cases) and males (302 cases). Most of these cases involved children. This was a hundred years before American physicians discovered child abuse.

Even during his time, Ambroise Tardieu was unable to convince his peers regarding the prevalence of child abuse (sexual or otherwise) within society and their own families. His successors in the field of forensic medicine also did not pay heed to allegations of sexual and physical abuse made by children. Instead, victims of child sexual abuse were forced to suffer neglect and abuse for another century with no support from the medical community.

Public concern regarding child sexual abuse only gained momentum in the 1970s and 1980s. Previously, child sexual abuse had been a socially unspeakable phenomenon and until the 1920s, there were no studies addressing this horrific reality. The first national estimate for the prevalence of child abuse was published in 1948. In the 20 years that followed, 44 of 50 U.S. states enforced laws that made it mandatory for physicians to file reports for any cases where child abuse was suspected. The Child Abuse, Prevention, and Treatment Act were enforced in 1974. That same year, the National Center for Child Abuse and Neglect was also created. The number of reported child abuses cases has increased significantly since then. In 1979, the National Abuse Coalition was also created to put pressure on Congress regarding the creation of more sexual abuse laws.

Public awareness regarding child sexual abuse and violence against women increased also due to second wave feminism. In 1986, the Child Abuse Victims' Rights Act was passed, which gave children civil rights in sexual abuse cases. With more laws created in the next two decades regarding the prosecution and detection of child molesters, the change in attitude can be accurately defined as one of history's biggest social revolutions.

Sadly, increased public awareness has not exactly managed to curb these monsters. Child molesters can be found everywhere and even the most unlikely of people may be guilty of committing this crime.

Who Can Be a Child Molester?

If you're wondering about there being some kind of set boundary for a child molester, the answer is no. There is not. A child molester can come from any kind of economic background or geographic area. They can be found in every race, ethnicity and creed. The only thing that is common among these individuals is that they have thoughts about sexual interactions with a child and that they act on these thoughts.

If we try to define who can be a child molester, then we would have the following conclusions:

- ✓ A child molester can be of any gender. 88% of these individuals are male, while 9% of them are females. The remaining 3% are unknown.
- ✓ A child molester can be of any age, can belong to any socioeconomic group and can hold any kind of occupation. You will find child molesters among the young and the old; they can be wealthy or belong to the middle class. They may even be disadvantaged.

Are They Only Strangers?

Child molestation is not limited to strangers. In reality, a large percentage of child sexual abuse occurs on the hand of a family member. 49% of the victims abused by a family member are younger than 6 years old. 42% of the victims are between the ages of 7 and 11 and 24% of the victims are between 12 to 17 years old.

In the case of young children that get abused, the fact remains that given their age, the perpetrator is likely to be a family member.

Are They Only Males?

As for the myth that only males can be sex offenders, this is also not true. As stated earlier, female offenders have also been held responsible for child sexual abuse and 9% of child molestation cases have a female as the perpetrator. 12% of their victims are less than 6 years old, while 6% of them are between the ages of 6-12.

What About Kids?

When we think of child molesters, we are likely to think of an adult male or female. However, based on substantial reports, one-third of childhood sexual abuse is committed by kids and teens. The average on-set age of such behavior in kids is 12-14 years old. Some of these juvenile offenders also have a history of being sexually abused themselves. However, a majority of the victims of sexual abuse do not go on to become sex offenders later in life.

How Many in the United States?

Currently, there are 847,725 individuals living in the United States that are registered child molesters. These are the people who were caught and convicted. They served their time and now they live amongst us.

This number discounts those child molesters who are currently serving their sentence. Additionally, as per the FBI, only 10% of child molestation cases are actually reported. This means that there are still millions of child molesters living right in the United States, most of who have not been caught.

How Many in Other Countries?

Child sexual abuse is prevalent across the world. Based on a 2007 study of ten countries in Africa, 19.6 percent of girls and 21.1 percent of boys between the ages of 11 and 16 years reported that they had experienced sexual abuse. The rates were even higher for 16 year olds, with 28.8 percent of girls and 25.4 percent of boys having experienced sexual abuse.

In India, a 2007 study on child abuse that interrogated 12,447 children, 2,324 young adults and 2,449 others in 13 states reported an overwhelming amount of child sexual abuse, with 53.2 percent of the participants saying they had been molested at least once in their life. Among these, 52.94 percent of the victims were boys, while 47.66 percent of the victims were girls. The most number of child sexual abuse cases were in Andhra Pradesh, Bihar, Assam, and Delhi.

If you move to the Pacific, child sexual abuse is also prevalent in Papua New Guinea, with 50 percent of rape victims being younger than 15 years and 13 percent under 7 years.

In the United Kingdom, a study conducted in 2010 estimated that 5 percent of boys and 18 percent of girls had been subjected to child sexual abuse. What's more, between 2009 and 2010, a total of 23,000 child molestation cases were reported.

On a global scale, the prevalence of child sexual abuse presents a grim picture indeed. It doesn't matter whether you are white, black, or brown, belong to an affluent family or to a poor one, speak English, or any other language—child sexual abuse surpasses all geographic and ethnic boundaries. A collective effort is needed to uproot this evil from society and provide our children with a safe environment to grow in.

Chapter 2

Profiling a Child Molester

Profiling and understanding the mind of a child molester is important, not because we hope to attain a sense of empathy for them or help them, but because it is essential to understand their thinking and behavioral patterns in order to identify them and get them arrested and convicted.

As understood earlier, a child molester will treat children as the object of their sexual fantasies. They also tend to rationalize the idea of having a sexual interest in children. Child molesters have very predictable behavioral patterns. They have excellent interpersonal skills, especially with children. This allows them to come across as charming and win over the trust of a child.

Child molesters are likely to target kids that appear to be loners or those who are neglected and troubled in some way.

Kinds of Child Molesters

There are two main types of child molesters. The first is a situational child molester; the second is a preferential child molester.

A situational child molester is someone who "doesn't have a true sexual interest in children". They will use children for sexual stimulation when some kind of stress has been introduced in their life. These individuals have comparatively fewer victims. They also do not limit themselves to only children and will take advantage of the elderly as well as those who are mentally impaired.

Situational child molesters can be divided into further subtypes. There is the regressed child molester, who is compelled by some sort of incident to sexually exploit children. Acts of child sexual abuse performed by these individuals are an abnormal occurrence and these individuals will normally prefer adults. They use children as an outlet of their stress and usually feel more comfortable with them. In terms of social profile, they are likely to be employed, and have a stable lifestyle. They have some history of substance abuse, however, and may also have a low self-esteem.

The second type of situational child molester is the morally indiscriminate kind. This person will abuse people of all ages, and children are unfortunately included among their victims. They are interested in sexual experiments and may target their own children in these experiments due to easy access.

There is also a third and final subtype for a situational child molester, referred to as the naïve or inadequate molester. Individuals belonging to this type tend to be mentally incapacitated. They are unable to distinguish between right and wrong and will unwittingly target children. These individuals usually tend to be loners, although not by choice and simply because they are incapable of having normal personal relationships with other people. Another prominent behavioral characteristic is that unlike other types of molesters, they will not harm children. Any exploitation will involve, holding, kissing, fondling, or licking. They do not coerce children into sexual intercourse or even oral and anal sex. They will molest children simply because they view them as non-threatening and hence, prefer children to adults. They may also have a collection of pornography, but they do not watch pornography that features children.

A preferential child molester is one who, unlike the situational child molester, will habitually abuse children for their sexual gratification. They can be further classified under two subtypes.

The first kind is the Mysoped child molester and killer. These individuals are sadists and connect sexual gratification with violence. They are usually male and will target victims outside of their family. Instead of seduction, they are likely to stalk children instead and take them by force. They will abduct children from schools, playgrounds, shopping centers and any other places where children gather in large numbers. They have no sympathy or love for their victims and are only fixated on causing them harm and eventually killing them. Their acts tend to be premeditated and they will follow a particular set of rituals.

Albert Fish was one of these monsters. For those readers who are unaware, Fish was an American serial killer and child rapist. He was also a cannibal. Three of his known victims were Francis McDonell (8 years old), Billy Gaffney (11 years old), and Grace Budd (10 years old). He was also suspected of murdering 5 other children who were between the ages of 5 and 17.

The second kind of preferential child molester is the Fixated child molester. These individuals do not interact much with people of their own age. They are usually single and are considered to be immature and are uncomfortable around people their own age. This kind of molester often exhibits childlike behavior and likes children because they appear to be less demanding, are easy to dominate and also because they don't criticize them like adults. Unlike the first kind, these molesters do not want to harm children. They will seduce them buying them gifts and then try to get intimate with the child. They will initially get the child to perform only oral-genital sex. Proper sexual intercourse happens after a very long period of time.

Gaining Access to Victims

Child abuse can be opportunistic in nature, but preferential child molesters who have built a lifestylearound sexual exploitation of children will have common strategies that allow them access to victims. These can range from befriending parents, offering to babysit children, taking jobs that involve interacting with children, becoming a foster parent or guardian, spending time in places where children are present such as playgrounds and parks, and using the internet to lure kids.

The internet, in particular, is full of these predators. They will target unsuspecting youngsters and lure them through attention and flattery. They will often target adolescents who feel lonely and neglected. The issue becomes considerably serious if they manage to obtain the personal information of the victim such as their full name, address, and phone number. These cyber predators can convince their victims to meet them in person and will eventually rob, assault or sexually abuse them. If they manage to convince their victims to share intimate videos or pictures, then they also resort to sextortion, where they use these images to blackmail them for more images.

The Very Important Persons

Child sexual abuse is also connected to what is called as the "VIP Factor". These are the people in powerful positions such as local leaders in schools, houses of worship, business and healthcare communities, and athletic and civic organizations. As a result of their position, as well as the money they have, they are able to impose a culture of silence and their crimes go unreported.

Jerry Sandusky, an assistant coach at Penn State University, is one example of this. Sandusky was charged with 48 sexual crimes against children and he was convicted of 45 of these. His victims were usually 8-12 year old boys who did not have fathers. He used affection, authority, bribery, games, hero worship, jobs, threats, weapons, drugs, and assistance to lure and sexually exploit his victims.

Places of Assault

Most children tend to get sexually abused within the premises of their own home, the home of the molester, or someone else's residence. 81 percent of child abuse incidents involve one molester vs. one child. In the case of juvenile child molesters, most cases will happen within school premises between 3 and 7 PM, with a majority happening between 3 and 4 PM.

Difference Between a Pedophile and a Child Molester

There is a lot of confusion regarding the terms pedophile and child molester. A lot of people even consider a pedophile and a child molester to be synonymous with each other. However, not all pedophiles are child molesters. A pedophile is a person with a sexual preference for children. They may fantasize about having sexual intercourse with children, but if they do not act on these preferences, then they cannot be called a child molester.

Some pedophiles also act on their fantasies in legal ways. These include simply watching or talking to children and masturbating later. Some may have sex with mannequins and dolls that resemble children. They may also have sex with adults who look, dress, or act like young children. They can also act out fantasy games with an adult prostitute or an online partner.

Eventually, you cannot arrest and prosecute people simply for their fantasies. You must also consider that while all pedophiles are not child molesters, this works the other way around too—not all child molesters are pedophiles. A person who generally prefers to engage in sex with an adult partner may also decide to molest a child. This may be due to opportunity, availability, a desire to hurt someone close to the child, or curiosity.

Can a Vigilant Parent Detect a Child Molester?

Unfortunately, even if you are a vigilant parent, detecting a child molester can be hard. This is because most child molesters are excellent at gaining the trust of children and their parents. Many of them attempt to get involved in the child's life by interacting with their family and making contact with the child at their school, house of worship, etc. The child molester may join the child in playing sports or other hobbies.

This makes it easier for them to gain their trust. They will often be ready to babysit your child or drive them to places. You cannot expect a child molester to quiver with shame or guilt before your eyes. Instead, they will smile, look you right in the eye and convince you of their trustworthiness. In a lot of cases, a child may also be molested by a close family member or someone you have known for a significant period of time. Given the natural trust you feel towards such individuals, it can be hard to determine their true intentions.

Myth vs. Fact
Myth – There is a common notion that child molesters are people who look distrustful and suspicious.

Fact –Child molesters are masters of deception. They can be overly confident, rich, pretty, and wholesome individuals that you like.

Myth – A child molester prefers loneliness and isolation.

Fact – While some child molesters may live in isolation, a vast majority of them tend to have a friendly and lively persona. They have great interpersonal skills and blend in anywhere. Considering that their isolation would not really allow them to get near children, you can see why they project this image.

Myth – A child molester is likely to be someone with a low income, in between jobs, and may have a low level of intelligence.

Fact – Child molestation cannot be defined through the kind of life a person leads. It is primarily caused due to a mental issue or a behavioral disorder. As mentioned earlier, the smartest, wealthiest, and the most influential members of your community can also be child molesters. In fact, statistically speaking, a majority of child molestation cases involve educated, white men.

Profiling and understanding the mind of a child molester can be a difficult process. Most of us cannot even fathom the idea of being sexually attracted to children, let alone using them for sexual gratification. However, knowing their basic profile is the first step in identifying a child molester and stopping them from committing these heinous acts.

Chapter 3

Child Sexual Abuse: Effects and Treatment

Child sexual abuse is characterized by physical and psychological effects that cause harm in the short and the long-term. Despite the prevalence of child sexual abuse cases, for a long time, there was little emphasis on the psychological impact of this form of abuse. There was more concern regarding the resulting physical harm as well as damage to the child's reputation.

The Psychological Effects of Child Sexual Abuse

Psychological indicators and effects of child sexual abuse include depression, eating disorders, anxiety, sleep disturbance, somatization, poor self-esteem and dissociative disorders like post-traumatic stress disorder. Victims of child sexual abuse may isolate themselves, withdraw from any social activities, and showcase behavioral and learning difficulties. They may also show cruelty to animals. Child sexual abuse victims are also known to inflict self-harm.

Behavioral problems in victims of child sexual abuse can include Attention deficit hyperactivity disorder, Conduct disorder and Oppositional defiant disorder. The Attention deficit hyperactivity disorder, also known as ADHD, is characterized by hyperactivity and the inability to control your impulses. Children suffering from this disorder have trouble paying attention. Conduct disorder is another behavioral and emotional disorder in children where the child displays violent and disruptive behavior. Finally, the oppositional defiant disorder is characterized by persistent or frequent patterns of irritability, anger, defiance, confrontation, or vindictiveness towards parents or other authority figures.

These issues can go on to impact a child's relationships with family and friends and can cause problems in their adult life too.

A causal relationship has also been found between child sexual abuse and several adult psychopathologies, including alcoholism, drug abuse, crime, and suicide. Males who have been sexually abused as children are more likely to commit crimes later in life.

Child sexual abuse can impact future generations as well as children whose parents were victims of child sexual abuse. These children show more behavioral and emotional problems than their peers and have difficulty fitting in.

Victims of chronic sexual abuse also develop dissociative symptoms like amnesia, where they don't have any memories of the abuse.

The Physical Effects of Child Sexual Abuse

Physical effects of child abuse include injuries such as bleeding and internal lacerations. Severe cases also involve damage to internal organs. It can result in infections due to the lack of sufficient vaginal fluid in young girlsand can also cause the child to suffer from sexually transmitted diseases.

Child sexual abuse can also cause neurological damage and may have a deteriorating effect on brain development. Some studies also show the effects of sexual and physical abuse to cause damage to the Limbic system of the child. Damage to the limbic system can affect a child's ability to store information in their conscious memory and can cause short-term memory impairments.

Why Do Most Victims Not Tell Someone About Being Abused?

Nine out of ten children will not tell anyone about being sexually abused. This may be due to multiple reasons. Firstly, the abuser can be a family member on whom the child depends upon for things like food and shelter. They may also still love this individual and might not want to see them in trouble. They may also believe that disclosing about their abuse may break up the family. In other cases, the abuser may have threatened them; hence, they feel afraid of what the abuser might do if they tell someone.

A lot of survivors of sexual abuse also feel a sense of embarrassment, guilt and shame over what happened. They believe that they were responsible and did something that caused the abuse. For example, a child with a carefree nature who mingles easily with adults may believe that it was their behavior that somehow encouraged the abuser.

It is absolutely vital to note here that the fault NEVER lies with the child.

Treatment

Treating a person with a history of sexual abuse depends upon factors like the age at which they disclosetheir abuse, the circumstances of disclosure, and the presence of comorbid conditions (the presence of an additional disease(s) or disorder(s)occurring alongside a primary disorder or disease.

There are three kinds of therapy suggested for treatment— family therapy, individual therapy, and group therapy. The kind of treatment chosen varies from case to case. If the child is young, then parents are likely to play a more prominent role, and family therapy may be the best option. Adolescents, on the other hand, are more independent and in this case, individual or group therapy may be suitable.

Treatment will also vary according to the severity and type of sexual abuse, the frequency and the age at which it occurred.

Adults with a history of childhood sexual abuse are often treated for secondary mental health issues as well such as substance abuse, depression, personality disorders, eating disorders, or difficulties in interpersonal and romantic relationships.

The treatment varies according to the case. In some cases, due to a more deep-seated nature of the trauma, cognitive restructuring may be a good option. New techniques like eye movement desensitization and reprocessing (EMDR) have also proven to be effective. This is a form of psychotherapy that allows individuals to recover from emotional distress resulting from disturbing life experiences.

There is no set formula for the effects and treatment of child sexual abuse. However, with the right support, encouragement and initiatives taken to protect our children from any further incidences, there is some hope of alleviating the damage caused. Family, in particular, plays a very important role to ensure the long-term benefits of treatment and can help prevent a relapse of symptoms.

Chapter 4
The Reality of the Deep Web

Believe it or not, the Deep Web is a real thing and not a figment of a hacker's overactive imagination. It won't show up on search engines and is essentially a hidden part of the Web. The sites hosted are password protected and if you want to become a member, then you need to be invited. It is used by drug dealers, but for the most part, it is populated by pedophiles— a lot of them.

An undergrad student attempted to penetrate into this online community as part of her research project and the discoveries she made will leave you horror-struck.

The Dark Web is home to an entire community of pedophiles. They have a system in place that enables them to find each other. For instance, child pornographers have their own equivalent of Wikipedia. It is titled "Hard Candy," and it is only accessible on the Dark Web. In her research, the student came across a heavily guarded website called 7axxn. Membership required getting an invite from a current member and if you wanted to gain their trust, you had to break the law by providing, for example, a link to child pornography.In fact, some forums on the Dark Web only let new members enter if they submit an applicationcontaining examples from their personal child pornography library.

By sheer luck (not by breaking the law and downloading child pornography), the undergrad student was able to get an invite. The things she came across were nothing short of terrifying.

The people present on the Dark Web are those who have dedicated themselves to victimizing and raping children while also figuring out new ways to do it. 7axxn alone has more than 90,000 registered users. While some of them are there for the porn (how comforting), there are those who take part in active discussions regarding child sexual abuse, conduct polls, and dissect the popularity of things like pornography, which features children being subjected to violent physical abuse. They refer to it as "Hurtcore" and give their views as though they are discussing the best way to fight global warming or whether a movie deserved the Emmy it won.

Other charming highlights of their discussions include debates like the benefits of drugging children before you rape them, and believe it or not, one of the opinions that the student came across was, "Drugs are not necessary since children are heavy sleepers."

The practical tone prevalent throughout most of these discussions is enough to make you want to kill yourself. There's also a notable divide between the pedophile communities on these sites. There are those who are at peace with the idea that they have sexually assaultedchildren, and then there are those who call themselves child *lovers.* These child lovers believe that they simply exist in a mutually sexual relationship with someone who just happens to be a 5 year old.

One of the moderators on 7axxn who goes by the name Sarah claims that she has three children who she and her husband rape on a regular basis while convincing them that is normal and a source of enjoyment. Her husband is a member on 7axxn too and they claim that they are "bringing up their children as pedo".

According to this woman, she was molested as a child by her dad and enjoyed the experience so much that she now takes pride in being a pedophile. She had always planned on having kids that she could later molest and obviously could not find her Mr. Right the normal way. She then spent time on pedo chat rooms where she met Brian, the man of her dreams. They got married after three months. As if this isn't sickening enough, Sarah and Brian have actually laid out some rules as well. These are things like no sexual contact before their child is 5 years old; if anything makes their children uncomfortable, they will not continue it and their children are free to say no; there would be no physical punishment, including spanking, andsex would not be used as a punishment (neither would withholding sex); they would never lie to their kids and they would never censor anything from their kids.

Of course, Sarah and Brian admit to have violated the first rule immediately after their daughter was born. She claims her children to be willing participants. The entire logic set up by these child lovers is sickeningly bizarre and with loopholes that suit them. They insist that continuing to have sexual intercourse with a child after they say no is bad, but then they go around their "rule" and condition the child's mind from birth so that they never say no because the child doesn't know what their parents are doing to them and believe that such acts are normal.

If you're wondering how people like Sarah and Brian manage to brag about their activities on the web without getting caught, well, that's because among other things, these pedophiles are initially aided by a handbook. The handbook contains arguments justifying pedophilia as just another sexual orientation. It also provides tips like buying child porn in Bitcoin, how to have sexual intercourse with children while hiding it from the people around them, etc. There are hints for newbie pedophiles to write CP instead of child pornography and referto their victims as "young friends". The community also protects itself, making sure it only uses browsers like Tor that help keep their communication anonymous and untraceable. They also have very vigilant moderators.

As sick as these individuals are, they take particular care in never mentioning their location. They are also warned to never answer polls asking for survey data. The undergrad student looked as hard as she could for any evidence that could be admissible in court, but there was nothing. To put it simply, the pedophile community on the Deep Web is completely open about the ways they want to abuse and torture children and they are also equally careful about hiding their location and any other data that can be traced back and used to identify them.

The browser they use (Tor), also offers them plenty of protection. It was originally designed for the government to carry out communications that could not be traced, but like so many other things, this too has only done more damage than good and helped these monsters.

Chapter 5

Beyond Conviction

Child molestation is a very serious criminal offence in the United States, and the justice system takes a stringent approach towards child molesters. It is considered a felony in all fifty states of the US, punishable through several penalties.

If convicted of child molestation, the perpetrator will have to serve a jail term. The period served varies from state to state and can be one year to thirty years for a first time offender. The amount of time served depends on factors such as the age of the child and the child molester's criminal history. If the child is younger than 14 years of age, the jail term is likely to be longer. The severity of the sentence is increased in case of repeat offenses and in some states, a child molester who is repeatedly convicted of this crime can either get a life sentence or a death penalty.

Besides the jail term, child molesters can also be fined. They may be ordered by the court to do community service and undergo counseling. The child victim can also file a civil lawsuit against the child molester and seek compensation for damages.

Beyond the legal consequences, there are other ramifications to child molestation as well. Firstly, a child molester must live with the stigma attached to the crime for the rest of their lives. They will also be shunned by society and their friends and family will no longer want to be associated with them. Even after they have served time, theircriminalrecord will be public knowledge and can be accessed by anyone who does a background check. This will make things like getting a job and renting an apartment very difficult. A child molester is also required to get registered in the state's sex offender database. This database is accessible by anyone. Failing to register in the state's sex offender database is also a criminal offense.

The Jimmy Ryce Act

The Jimmy Ryce Act aims at reviewing inmates having a history of sexual offense by the Florida Department of Corrections, the Florida Department of Children and Families, and state attorneys who determine the level of risk associated with these individuals and the likelihood that they will repeat their crimes.

The act was formed after the brutal rape and murder of Jimmy Ryce in 1995. Jimmy Ryce was only nine years old when he was abducted barely a block away from his home. Juan Carlos Chavez, the man convicted of his rape and murder, confessed that he had blocked Jimmy's path as he was on his way home with his pickup truck. He held him at gunpoint and forced Jimmy into the truck and took him to his trailer where he raped Jimmy. Four hours later when Jimmy heard the sound of a helicopter, he ran to the door of the trailer and tried to open it, at which point, Chavez shot him in the back. He then decapitated Jimmy and also dismembered him. Jimmy's dismembered and decapitated body was discovered near Chavez's trailer after 3 months. In 1998, Chavez was found guilty of sexual battery, kidnapping, and capital murder. He was given a death penalty and was executed by lethal injection on the eve of February 12,

2014. This was 19 years after the original crime took place.

In light of what happened to Jimmy, the Jimmy Ryce Act was passed in Florida. It became effective in 1999.

According to the act, inmates convicted of sexual offenses are subject to civil proceedings. They are also committed to a secure facility for treatment after their release. The treatment facility had received much criticism for ineffective treatment and poor security. It was also found to be understaffed and underfunded.

The Cherish Periwinkle Case

In 2013, Cherish Periwinkle, an eight-year-old girl, was kidnapped from a Walmart store in Jacksonville, Florida. She was then murdered. In the trial that followed, James Donald Smith was seen as the perpetrator. He had been on caught on the surveillance cameras in Walmart and was seen leaving the parking lot with Cherish in his car. When the authorities managed to hunt him down, he stated that Cherish had been in his car very briefly and jumped out at a red light. Evidence suggested otherwise and Smith was arrested. Officials were even more frustrated when they discovered that Smith was a registered sex offender as well. In 2014, Florida was among the top 10 states having a high population of sex offenders. Studies also showed that 70 percent of these convicted sexual predators will commit similar crimes after their release. This is only the portion of child molesters that have been convicted. Post the murder of Cherish Periwinkle, there was an increased amount of focus on existing laws for sexual predators. Legislators in Florida agreed that there should be harsher penalties for these sexual predators. Changes were also made to the Jimmy Ryce Act and other laws related to sexual offenses.

Changes Made to the Jimmy Ryce Act

Under previous laws, convicted sexual offenders underwent a reevaluation process before they were released. If they failed this evaluation, they were simply transferred to the Florida Civil Commitment Center. State attorneys stated that this evaluation process required increased funding to provide more accurate results. Revisions in the Jimmy Ryce Act aimed at changing this evaluation process and making it increasingly stringent so that offenders who show an inclination towards repeating their crimes don't get off so easily. The probationary period for sexual offenders transferred to the Jimmy Ryce facility was also extended. Lawmakers proposed that these individuals should be under lifetime supervision of the state, which meant that the probationary period could continue indefinitely. Therefore, they would not be able to enter into society without being under community supervision.

Penalties for Failure to Report Child Molestation

Failing to report child abuse comes with its own set of penalties and nearly 48 states impose penalties on individuals who willfully fail to report a case of suspected child abuse. Florida considers it to be a felony, while 40 other states consider it as a misdemeanor. In Minnesota and Arizona, the misdemeanor charge can be upgraded to a felony if an individual fails to report a particularly serious situation involving child abuse. Connecticut, Kentucky, Illinois, and Guam consider a second violation of this law as a felony.

If an individual is convicted of this charge, then they can face a jail term of 30 days or 5 years. A fine can also be charged, which ranges between $300 and $10,000. In some states, the individual may also be held liable under damages caused by their inaction.

Institutions of higher learning are slapped with higher fines in case of non-reporting. This includes non-public colleges, as well as State universities. In Florida, this fine is up to $1 million.

10 US states also impose penalties on employers who attempt to prevent employees or a volunteer from reporting a case of suspected child abuse. Six states consider it a misdemeanor. In Connecticut, it is considered a felony. In Maryland, an employer who tries to prevent a report is charged with 5 years in jail or fined $10,000. Penalties in Wyoming involve 6 months in jail and a fine of $750. Minnesota, Oklahoma, Vermont, and North Dakota also consider the employer liable to pay damages for the harm caused to due to their actions.

Child Molesters in Prison

Prisons follow a hierarchy of sorts. A person charged with murder or robbery will likely be towards the top of this hierarchy. Rapists and child molesters, on the other hand, occupy the bottom. Most inmates tend to have families, so even though they have been convicted, they follow a code of honor in terms of victims and criminal offenses. Since women are considered to be weak, a rapist is automatically looked down upon. A child molester is considered even worse.

While awaiting trial in the country jail, child molesters are usually segregated and grouped together in one general area. Once they get sentenced, they will be transferred to a correctional facility, where they are placed among the general population. Given how even convicted criminals view these child molesters, life in prison is extremely hard. In the south, prisoners refer to these child molesters as "Tree Jumpers", because they are considered to be individuals who jump out and grab children. In the north, prisoners call them "Short Eyes".

They are viewed as sick freaks by their inmates and considered untouchable. Everyone, from the inmates to the guards, hates a child molester, and they are often set up for beatings because they deserve it. Inmates may also charge them rent for staying in the cell block. Besides beatings, a child molester is also subjected to rape and assault as a form of retribution.

There have been several cases where inmates who felt that a prison sentence was not enough for the crime committed and took matters into their own hands. One child molester was forcibly tattooed on the forehead with the name of his victim. Another one was killed by his inmates.

A child molester will usually try his best to not reveal his crime to fellow inmates. However, inmates may ask their families who visit them to do a background check on someone they feel suspicious of. If they find out that an inmate is indeed a child molester, things can take an extremely unpleasant turn.

Incidents in Prison

There have plenty of notable cases where inmates are banded together to seek retribution from child molesters. When ten-year-old Katie Collman was raped and murdered, the police arrested Anthony Ray

Stockelman among a few others for the crime. Katie had witnessed Stockelman and his friends making methamphetamine and paid a brutal price.

Stockelman was sentenced to life in prison for his crimes, but his fellow inmates at Wabash Valley Correctional Facility in Indiana did not think that was punishment enough. Among those inmates was 22-year-old Jared Harris, who just so happened to be a distant cousin of Katie's and knew what Stockelman had done.

After repeatedly threatening him, Harris came into Stockelman's cell one evening and threatened him with two options— a tattoo or death. Naturally, Stockelman chose the tattoo. Using a makeshift tattoo gun, Harris then proceeded to carve a tattoo on Stockelman's forehead that read "KATIE'S REVENGE".

Stockelman was removed to a secluded area of the prison once the tattoo was discovered by the prison staff. This is one of the many cases where inmates took matters into their own hands and gave punishments to rapists and child molesters.

In 2014, Daryell Dickson Menenzes Xavier went to prison for raping his one-year-old stepson. The boy was admitted to a hospital but succumbed to his injuries. Xavier then admitted his crime and claimed that he had been under the influence of 'Satan'. When his inmates found out what he had done, Xavier was attacked and raped twice.

There was another incident in 2012 where a man by the name of Mitchell Harrison went to prison after being convicted of raping and murdering a 13-year-old girl. He had also been caught behaving inappropriately with a 15-year-old and a 7-year-old. In line with the previous incidents, Harrison was also attacked by his inmates with razor blades and shanks. They stabbed and disemboweled him and killed him in the process.

Scope for Rehabilitation

There are several methods employed to help rehabilitate child molesters and prevent them from repeating their crime. Some states opt for chemical castration of child molesters and offer an early release. This is believed to reduce their sexual desire for children. However, I believe this to be ineffective because pleasure and satisfaction felt by a child molester are not limited to sexual acts. For instance, in one of the cases I worked on in Florida, a person was arrested for sucking on the toes of a child living in his neighborhood. Since this is not typically a sexual act, he would have been charged with Battery. However, he admitted to Law Enforcement that the act made him feel sexually aroused. In light of this admission, he was charged with child molestation instead.

In some cases, the charges do not stick because they do not have a sexual connotation attached. I had a case where an offender was caught in his home with adult pornographic photographs. What he had done was cut out the faces of small children and taped them onto the bodies of the adult pornographic photographs. We tried to get him charged with the photos, but since the bodies were of adult women, the state attorney could not move forward with the case and we had to let him go.

Group therapy is also considered as a potential form of treatment for these individuals.

Aversion therapy has also been considered. This involves pairing an unpleasant stimulus such as a pinch, electric shock, or flick with a pleasant stimulus as sexual desire.

In my personal opinion, however, and especially after having worked with child molesters in correctional facilities, there is no cure or treatment for these predators and what they do to children. In my professional opinion (and this may sound harsh, but it's true), the only way to cure them is with a bullet to the head.

Chapter 6

What Can We Do?

Child molesters are a very real threat to our society. As I have mentioned before, they can exist within the most normal of families and can come from any kind of social background, ethnicity, creed and gender.

Bearing these facts in minds, we, as responsible individuals of society, must seek to protect our children from these monsters. The statistics regarding the number of child molesters in the system and those who are yet to be caught are alarming and it is vital that we take the required measures to keep them at bay.

Protecting Our Children
The first step to protecting our children from sexual abuse is by teaching them about their bodies, particularly about their private body parts. Teaching children the names of body

parts from an early age is very important. They must know what their chest, buttocks, breasts, vagina, vulva, testicles, and penis are. Children also need to be told of their rights, they need to be educated about the control they have on their body. They must also be given a choice to accept or reject any kind of physical affection from someone. If a child refuses to let someone hug, touch or kiss them, we tend to scold the child. In doing so, we condition their minds to believe that refusing a person's attempt to touch them is 'bad behavior'. This only aids a child molester in their attempts to get close to and take advantage of a child. It is also why even when a child gets abused, they can't communicate the same to their parents because they fear that they will get scolded for 'being bad'.

Children also need to be educated that no one has the right to look, touch, or photograph their private body parts. They also need to know that no one can ask them to touch or look at someone else's body parts.

Besides education and awareness regarding their bodies, we also need to take the necessary steps required for our children to trust us with everything. It's important that you help your child choose at least two adults with their secrets. One of these adults should be at home and the other at school.

Additionally, we also need to trust our children. If a child tells you that a certain person makes them feel uncomfortable or gives them a funny feeling in their belly, then you must trust their instincts and act on them. Ignoring your child, even when they tell you how a certain person makes them uncomfortable, is effectively aiding a child molester. Even if you find the idea impossible to believe, do not leave your child alone with such a person. Additionally, keep an eye on them for signs of inappropriate behavior and report them to the authorities.

The National Sexual Assault Hotline

Besides taking protective measures at home, you must also learn a little about the National Sexual Assault Hotline. If you suspect or find out about a case of child sexual abuse, call 800.656.HOPE (4673). This will get you in touch with a trained staff member, who can provide you with confidential support. They can provide you with resources that will help your child heal and recover and also help you locate a nearby healthy facility, which provides care for sexual assault survivors. Furthermore, they will also provide you with information regarding laws about sexual assault and any medical concerns.

It is a completely safe and confidential service.

Parting Note

Understanding the profile of a child molester and knowing the role we must play to prevent these monsters from harming our children is very important in safeguarding the interests of our children. If you have taken the time to read through this, then I hope you feel somewhat equipped on what to do if you detect or find out about a case of child molestation. As I said in the beginning, confronting that this issue exists in every society of the world is the first step. We cannot turn a blind eye to the plight of children who fall victim to these monsters on a daily basis.

My final word on the matter is this: If a child confides in you about someone behaving inappropriately with them or you notice something out of the ordinary on your own, then Act.

www.ingramcontent.com/pod-product-compliance
Lightning Source LLC
Chambersburg PA
CBHW071123030426
42336CB00013BA/2176